WANDERING SPIRITS

TRAVELING MARY SHELLEY'S *FRANKENSTEIN*

SELENA CHAMBERS

Special Limited Edition

TALLHAT
PRESS

"Letter 1" first appeared on *WeirdFictionReview.com*, 2013.
"Letter 2" first appeared on *WeirdFictionReview.com*, 2013.
"Letter 3" first appeared on *WeirdFictionReview.com*, 2013.
All three letters appeared in Issue 2 of the *Nonbinary Review*, 2014.

selenachambers.com
Twitter: @BasBleuZombie
Facebook.com/Twiggsnet

Cover and interior art © 2016 Yves Tourigny.
Editing, cover design, and layout by Yves Tourigny.
Original photos by Selena Chambers.

Broadsheet™ was designed in 2000 by Brian Willson (3IP).
Emily Austen™ was designed in 2001 by Brian Willson (3IP).

ISBN-10: 1533286957
ISBN-13: 978-1533286956

To Mary Godwin Shelley,
Respect

"Wandering spirits, if indeed ye wander, and do not rest in your narrow beds, allow me this faint happiness, or take me, as your companion, away from the joys of life."

—Victor Frankenstein

LETTER 1

Villa Diodati, Cologny, Lake Geneva, Switzerland

June 1, 20--

Dear R--;

I have only been in Geneva for one day, and am beginning to suspect that my simple notion of traveling in Mary Shelley's footsteps, and through them her novel Frankenstein, is leading me to an entirely different creature than I expected.

Villa Diodati, Cologny, Lake Geneva, Switzerland
June 1, 20—

Dear R—,

I have only been in Geneva for one day, and am beginning to suspect that my simple notion of traveling in Mary Shelley's footsteps, and through them her novel *Frankenstein*, is leading me to an entirely different creature than I originally sought.

Not three hours off the train, I jumped on a bus to Cologny and made a pilgrimage to Chemin de Ruth 9, the Villa Diodati and Le Parc Byron. Frankly, it is not as dynamic or inspiring as I had imagined. I wanted to see whether Shelley's geography still existed, or if it was now pure fantasy. Of course, two hundred years of progress was going to drastically change the landscape, but surely some essence of her environs remains?

Cologny, where Le Parc Byron resides, is on the eastern shore of Lake Geneva. It's a small green space punctuated with a giant boulder commemorating the "mad, bad, and dangerous to know" George Gordon, Lord Byron, poet of *Don Juan* and *Childe Harold*. The memorial rock flanks a historical marker informing tourists: "On this very spot, the story 'Frankenstein' was born. During the summer of 1816, the weather was atrocious, cold, and rainy spells alternating with violent thunder storms. At that time Byron, a 28 year old poet, was renting the villa Diodati situated to the left of this meadow."

While *Frankenstein* is mentioned, what the Parc Byron historical marker could have elaborated upon is that during the summer of 1816, its author, 18-year old Mary Shelley, arrived in Geneva for a second time with her poet-dreamer lover Percy Bysshe Shelley, their illegitimate son, William,[i] her step-sister Claire Clairmont, and a lot of emotional baggage. She had already been in a relationship with Percy for two years, had traveled Post-Napoleonic Europe, birthed and mourned her first child, dabbled in a somewhat irksome experimentation in free love, and upon her London homecoming, felt the shame of a tarnished reputation.

The *ménage à trois* were propelled back to Geneva, mostly by Shelley's desire for a poetic commune promised by a rendezvous between Claire and Byron, who had begun an affair upon the Shelleys' return in London. While Byron's enthusiasm for Claire had begun to taper off, he was impressed with Shelley's talent, and respectful of Mary's intelligence and philosophical legacy.[ii] Soon the clan became inseparable, and the Shelleys moved from the Hôtel d'Angleterre in Sécheron, to a small chalet named Montalègre, just a ten minute walk from Villa Diodati.[iii] There the party sailed Lake Geneva, read and discussed literature and philosophy, and explored the Genevan perimeter. It would be the happiest period in young Mary's life: "...every evening at about six o'clock, we sail on the lake, which is delightful," she wrote back to London, "...the tossing of the boat raises my spirits and inspires me with unusual hilarity.... [We] seldom return until ten o'clock, when as we approach the shore, we are saluted by the delightful scent of flowers and new mown grass, and the chirp of grasshoppers,...

"I feel as happy as a new-fledged bird, and hardly care what twig I fly to, so that I may try my new-found wings...."[iv]

The opportunity to test those wings came when the summer turned stormy: "The thunder storms that visit us are grander and more terrific than I have ever seen before. We watch them as they approach from the opposite side of the lake, observing the lightning play among the clouds..., and dart in jagged figures upon the piney heights of Jura, while...the sun is shining cheerily upon us...."[v]

When the storms actually arrived on the Lake, the group retreated to the Villa to read German ghost stories out loud, leading Byron to challenge all his guests to a phantasmagorical write-off. It is perhaps the most famous challenge in literary lore, resulting in the creation of two of supernatural fiction's greatest icons: the vampire[vi] and the misunderstood Creature. The party was stumped by the Gothic challenge. According to Mary, in her revisionist telling of the legend in her 1831 preface[vii]: "I busied myself *to think of a story*...to rival those which had excited us to this task....I thought and pondered— vainly....'Have you thought of a story?' I was asked each morning, and...I was forced to reply with a mortifying negative."[viii]

But subconsciously, Mary had been steeping all of her experiences until one night a conversation brought her subconscious to a boil: "Many and long were the conversations between Lord Byron and Shelley to which I was a devout but nearly silent listener. During one of these, various philosophical doctrines were discussed, and among others the nature of the principle of life,...[the] probability of its ever being discovered and communicated.... Perhaps a corpse would be reanimated; galvanism had given token of such things: perhaps the component parts of a creature might be manufactured, brought together, and endued with vital warmth."[ix]

That night she had a nightmare where she "...saw the pale student of unhallowed arts kneeling beside the thing he had put together."[x] The "thing" became reanimated with life and, horrified, the student abandoned him in his lab, hoping the experiment's success would inevitably fail. In his chambers, the student awakes to find peaking from the curtains "the yellow watery eye" of the Creature. Her story born, Mary won the contest and continued its encouraged composition until it was completed in Italy, nine months later.

As you well know, R——, I love this account. It is my favorite anecdote in literary history, and was for me a gateway to Romanticism and to wanderlust. Ever since I first fell in love with the Satanic School[xi] as a teen, my daydreams consisted of travel, and I grew up believing that Art was improved by gained experience. I guess you could say Romanticism was to me what travel was to Captain Walton, who "read with ardor the accounts of various voyages," and whose expedition that opens *Frankenstein* was to him "the favorite dream of his early years." The Romantics, Mary Shelley especially, drew directly upon their influences and surroundings to teach the reader awareness of the world *they are in*, which is lush with riches that cannot be quantified, sold, or traded. It can only be experienced.

I can hear you scoff at my cliché, but this is a point of view I find often eclipsed by modern life's sensorial substitutions. Remember when we saw the hunting dolphins at Bald Point, R——? All the HD deep sea documentaries on Netflix couldn't convey how ferocious and cunning their hunting behaviors really are. David Attenborough can narrate all he wants, but nothing can replace the *a posteriori* sensation of breaking and splashing water revealing a breaching and fishing dolphin five feet away. Despite nature shows' diligence to authenticity, something about the television screen's fourth wall keeps these animals cutesy. In real life, however, you realize you don't want an arm to wade into their fishing territory. No. These aren't dolphins you want to pet and hitch a fin-ride. They are hunters driven by urges and laws beyond your grasp; mess with them—well, you might find yourself with an albatross hanging around your neck, or absent a hand like our poor friend, Buster.

I digress. This accumulation and appreciation of the sublime was at Romanticism's core, and has carved glaciers and valleys into my outlook on life and art. But the hitch: although Mary and these poets experienced a lifetime before they were thirty, here I was at 28, having never left my homeland. I needed to flee—go forth and find sublimity. What better guide than *Frankenstein*.

Because the heart of the story is so stirring, it is easy to forget that the novel contains more than the bare bones of the mad scientist plot. The flesh and blood of Shelley's tale are travelogues set in and around Geneva, Ingolstadt, Rhine Valley, the Arctic Circle, and the United Kingdom. While the novel begins with an Arctic expedition off of St. Petersburg, the genesis of the story begins here where I sit.

The Villa remains privately owned, making the Parc a compromise between this perimeter and literary tourists. While its windows are open to Lake Geneva's breeze, its doors are closed to admirers, and discreetly hides behind stone gates and landscaping. All one sees is an exterior view of the subtle Baroque manor, painted a pale yellow with green shutters, with its impressive Corinthian columns and balcony overlooking the Lake.

Compared to an 1835 print, it seems unchanged. The two

adolescent trees that flank the left side of the house now tower above it and lean toward the Lake. The house's much celebrated English garden, one of the characteristics that enticed Byron to rent it, is still there and blooms lavender and aloe. What has most changed is the topiary border blocking romantic pilgrims from the residency, roping it off from other homes, and distancing it from the verdant rolling grounds that once led the young coterie to the Lake for rowing and aimless wandering.

Even so, beyond the grounds, the manor's elegance is constantly marred by modernity. While the park itself is a verdant hill glittering with purple, yellow, and white wildflowers, its unique location seems to attract cell-talking, pot-smoking teenagers who loaf about on concrete benches. The panoramic view of the Lake is interrupted by sleek, futuristic yachts, and clunky mechanical cranes.

At first, I was disappointed to not see inside the Villa. It makes me feel like one of the sensation-seeking tourists that would spy on Byron across the Lake with telescopes. But as I sit in this hazy field, I realize the interior would tell me nothing. It is the exterior that bares the tale. Here, before the Juras, her experiences over her teenage years steeped, boiled, and finally exploded from her mind and onto the page. This realization has driven home many things I subconsciously noted (*a priori*) in my youth, but knew nothing of as an adult. *Frankenstein* isn't just a tale about Man going too far, but a journal of a young woman's experience.

Seriously? R——, you won't believe me, but a storm is rolling in over the Jura Mountains. I can't help but pray for lightning to follow and strike down any of these surrounding trees; just so I can say I experienced in the same setting young Frankenstein's electric epiphany: "When I was about fifteen years old we had retired to our house near Belrive, when we witnessed a most violent and terrible thunderstorm.... I remained, while the storm lasted, watching its progress with curiosity and delight. As I stood at the door, on a sudden I beheld a stream of fire issue from an old and beautiful oak which stood about twenty yards from our house; and so soon as the dazzling light vanished, the oak had disappeared, and nothing remained but a blasted stump. When we visited it the next morning, we found the tree shattered in a singular manner. It was not splintered by the shock, but entirely reduced to thin ribbons of wood.... Before this I was not unacquainted with the more obvious laws of electricity. On this occasion a man of great research in natural philosophy was with us, and excited by this catastrophe, he entered on the explanation of a theory...on the subject of electricity and galvanism, which was at once new and astonishing to me."[xii]

While the bruit thunder that crackles through the Jura crags is strangely mellifluent, there are no oak splinters or jabbering natural philosophers here, just docile cows tinkling under the reverberations of their grass-grazing jaws. A few moments ago, a landscaper (lucky man) began to manicure the Villa's lawn. Despite the mower's mechanical cacophony, I tried to conjure with the wafting cut grass, the chirping birds, and the crescendoing storm a synesthetic trance where I saw Mary's ghost through time and space gazing at the Lake on the balcony. No luck.

Will this be all I uncover as I visit all the X's on Mary Shelley's map?

"When you are ready," the Creature told his maker on the Mer de Glace, "I shall appear." Perhaps I am not ready yet, and haven't quite deciphered the cartography to be fully explored. I fear the further I explore *Frankenstein*'s geography—physically and intellectually—that this novel's map will become an atlas. Before and after *Frankenstein*, a compass spins around Mary Shelley's journey through life—a journey that ends with a bloated but enigmatic X in 1851. What lies buried there waiting to be uncovered and rewarded is what these letters seek to reap. At some point, the experience, the gleaning, will appear. When I am ready—. [Ed: Blurred ink, rest of paragraph made indecipherable].

The storm has rolled from the mountains and over to the Lake. I must go. It is misting, and is ruining the ink. Before I sign off and put this in post, let me urge you to join me, and bring with you shovels and lanterns, and of course your passport.

Your Wandering Spirit,

S—

LETTER 2

Ingolstadt, Germany

June 5, 20—

Dear R——,

It has been several days since I wrote you from the Diodati grounds, and I now write you from Ingolstadt, Germany. The organization of my travels has taken an odd and somewhat scatological turn. I spent the day after I last wrote wandering around the streets of the little

Ingolstadt, Germany
June 5, 20—

Dear R—,

It has been several days since I wrote you from the Diodati
grounds, and I now write you from Ingolstadt, Germany. The
organization of my travels has taken an odd and somewhat
scatological turn. I spent the day after I last wrote wandering
Geneva proper, trying to determine the significance—if any—of
setting a novel such as *Frankenstein* here.

I have a few theories about Geneva being the birth of
Romanticism via its famous philosopher-son Jean-Jacques Rousseau, a
writer who heavily influenced the Diodati group and championed the
Alpine travel craze of the late eighteenth and early nineteenth
centuries. During the summer of 1816, Mary Shelley studied
Rousseau's work while Byron and Shelley embarked on a bit of
literary tourism by tracing famous passages and landmarks of the
author's life. It is an understatement to say that if his ghost was
lingering during those days, it lingers even more within the city via
statues and museums. However, a discussion of Rousseau at this point
in tracing the novel seems pre-mature, as his fingerprint is indented
more in the Creature's flesh than Victor's. The Creature was not
attached to Geneva at all, I realized, and with that thought it
occurred to me that I was focusing in varied ways too much on the
creator and not the creation, and decided to give up Geneva for a
while and head to Ingolstadt, the Bavarian city where the Creature
was born, specifically at the University of Ingolstadt.

Founded by Louis the Rich, Duke of Bavaria in 1472, the
University became the medical and scientific center of Europe.[xiii]
The Ingolstädter Alte Anatomie (Old Anatomy Building) was the
foremost establishment specializing in anatomy and biology. It is the
lone survivor of the University, which closed in 1800 to move to
Landshut, and is today known as The German Museum of the
History of Medicine in Ingolstadt.

Ingolstadt looks more like the model home neighborhood of the Gingerbread man than the breeding ground for mad science. Cobblestoned streets are lined with thin, pastel Baroque houses with playful modern rooftop accoutrements. That aside, the old city seems unchanged from the late eighteenth century the Creature ran away from, making its innocuous and darling streets more jarring in my expectations. Perhaps it was because the Universal films tinted my mind's eye with scenes of greyscale, overcasted gloom illuminated by lightning storms that I expected a damp, stark, and sparse village. Even so, it was here in this light and whimsical city that a young man defiled corpses and sewed them into a newborn man. Even Kenneth Branagh's attempt at a more faithful adaption (filmed inside and outside at the Old Anatomy Building) is lost in the auteur's cinematographic Gothic glaze.

When I came upon the grey door of the pollen-yellow Ingolstädter Alte Anatomie, panic set in that I had somehow become the punchline to a slip-media/time-stream gag devised by the Internet, Global Tracking, Mary Shelley, and probably the Illuminati. However, once I entered and saw a gold coin of Mary Shelley's face in the gift shop, I knew I had found my mark. The contents of Frankenstein's lab are never described, but one could easily furnish it with the museum's scientific artifacts. Filled with medical apparatus spanning from ancient Greece to modern day, the true highlight of the museum's collection is its second floor, the Anatomy Lecture Theatre, where Victor would have spent most of his classroom time at the university, and where perhaps the same cadavers he would have studied now stand on display. The progressive professors of Ingolstadt created a proto-plasticization method made of bone glue, linseed oil, wax, and earth pigments to color the veins that enabled them to keep a ready anatomical reference on hand, and to (albeit unknowingly) allow curious tourists, 200 years later, to see what those students, including the fictional Dr. Frankenstein, saw.

Here, young Victor studies for two years, where he masters chemistry, mechanics, physics, biology, and, most importantly, galvanism—the field marrying anatomy and electricity. These fields, combined with a self-taught education in alchemy, lead Victor to stumble upon a possible solution for creating life.

Driven by his theories, he locks himself up in an attic-room "...separated from all the other apartments by a galley and staircase, I kept my workshop of filthy creation,... The dissecting room and the slaughter house furnished many of my materials...."[xiv] Tracing Victor's laboratory in Ingolstadt is a vain task, as most of the surrounding campus area has been converted into urban spaces. The local high school is said to have been dormitories during the University's heyday, and it would be easy to see a pale, anemic, stress-ridden science student burning midnight oil in one of the high school's narrow windows. In any case, in this attic-room, he constructs his creation and, horrified by the results, hides from family and friends in his quarters until his baby brother's murder beckons him back to Geneva.

While Victor's more fleshy "materials" are better known in the construction of his Creature, Victor's success relies largely on technology provided by the University and the favor of an eccentric professor, M. Waldemar: "He took me into his laboratory and explained to me the uses of his various machines, instructing me as to what I ought to procure and promising me the use of his own when I should have advanced far enough in the science not to derange their mechanism."[xv] Those instruments promised by Professor Waldemar are on display, such as brass and tubular microscopes; gadgets with Steampunky names like "Mechanical 'dynamometer'" (a pendulum-looking scale that somehow measures the muscle strength in hands[xvi]); and medical oddities like cyclopean and Siamese baby skeletons, a skull that served as a phrenological textbook, an anatomy table that could have played a part in an off-screen scene where Victor first puts scalpel to flesh, and, perhaps most relevant, a galvanic battery.

Roughly the size of a shoe box, the "Improved Electric Magneto Machine," as its lid's labeling reads, is a wooden box housing brass gears and electrical strips that generated electricity through two copper coils connected to iron magnets that would be applied to the patient—all activated and propelled via a hand-crank.

While cinematic renderings of Frankenstein's lab abound, they have furnished our collective consciousness with a dungeon electrified by Tesla coils and machine-age contraptions. The museum artifacts at Alte Anatomie suggest a more eclectic and less ominous working environment with its small university-loaned instruments. The unimposing wooden-cased devices on display would need considerable improvement to present the ominous environment of the iconic "Frankenstein's Lab." Fittingly, such tinkering and modification happens to be what Frankenstein becomes notorious for on campus.

As for Ingolstadt itself, Shelley devotes very little page time to it. But Frankenstein's materialist education in Ingolstadt is important for its contrast with Romantic Geneva, which informs the backdrop for most of *Frankenstein*'s drama. Perhaps because the Villa Diodati was the nest where Mary first took flight, she preserved it within the book that was born there. Victor Frankenstein's childhood home is the Villa Belrive,[xvii] an allusion to the manor's original moniker, Belle Rive, before Lord Byron re-christened it, and occupies the same plot on the Lake as Diodati.

Whereas Victor waxes poetic about the iconic Mont Blanc looming over his hometown valley, his only description of Ingolstadt is upon his arrival, where he tersely describes "the high white steeple of the town" meeting his eyes, perhaps disappointed at a landmark that pales next to Geneva's high white alps. While unapparent this early in the novel, Ingolstadt establishes a pattern where Victor *cannot* practice science within Genevan environs.

This moral symbology is implicitly reverberated throughout Victor's geographical descriptions, and establishes an underlying morality that commands the novel. When Victor returns from Ingolstadt, his homecoming is tainted by the consequences of his scientific achievements abroad,[xviii] and he finds the idyllic Geneva haunting rather than comforting. Even so, later in the novel, when the Creature blackmails Victor into constructing a mate, Frankenstein flees to England, Scotland, and Ireland to attempt the deed. Geneva, and its surrounding nature, represents the core of Frankenstein's principles, and all locales outside of it, beginning with Ingolstadt, characterize the irreversible materialist corruption he has committed against the Sublime. This is a notion initiated in Germany, but isn't fully explored until Frankenstein's bloody homecoming, and his attempts to find reprieve in Chamonix at the glacial church of Mont Blanc. So, a homecoming I must recreate.

I could try and find a graveyard or two to mull around in, but I believe what I sought here has been found. I must catch the next train back to Geneva, traversing through the Black Forest with the Creature, who ventured westward for his own answers.

I shall be at the Manotel Royal if you need to reach me.

Until then,

S—

LETTER 3

Manotel Royal, Geneva, Switzerland

June 7, 20—

Dear R——,

I have been to Chamonix and Mont Blanc. I don't know if it is lack of oxygen from ascending the mountain, or the Bordot I imbibe while writing this, but I AM 39 minelated. I feel like I finally found what I was seeking. It would make sense that it would be at the Mer de Glace, since the Glace itself features so prominently in the

Manotel Royal, Geneva, Switzerland
June 7, 20—

Dear R—,

I have been to Chamonix and Mont Blanc. I don't know if it is lack of oxygen from ascending the mountain, or the Bandol I imbibe while writing this, but I'm elated. I feel like I finally found what I was seeking! It would make sense that it would be at the Mer de Glace, since the Glace itself features so prominently in the book's scenery.

Frankenstein has been popularly characterized as a parable against man playing God, presuming that there was a God who made man; however, the theological views of its author do not support such an interpretation. Mary Shelley came from a famously atheist family, and married an even more notorious skeptic. But, even so, there is within *Frankenstein* a looming mysticism stemming from Romanticism's concept of sublimity.

While the other Romantic poets such as Coleridge and Wordsworth regarded nature as the glorious evidence of a Christian God, Percy perceived a nourishing and destructive force reflective of man's imagination. His ode "Mont Blanc: Lines Written in the Vale of Chamouni [sic]"[xix] expresses this view and replaces religion with nature, establishing a moral code that Mary expands upon in *Frankenstein*'s later editions.

Creation is a monstrous act. Be it success or failure—it can be something suddenly in the world when a few seconds before it was not—it could be beautiful, it could be hideous, but most importantly it now exists—and the consequences of its existence can be quite substantial. There are myriad ways to interpret *Frankenstein*, but this is its essence—its germ of suggestion, and its mass appeal anchor. All too often, we callously create while lacking the foresight or understanding to realize that, once our creation is in the world, it is out of our control. This is true of art, of philosophy, of parenthood, and of government. The creature you make may break you.

While it may seem like hyperbole, *Frankenstein* illustrates examples of all of these aspects and pulls into focus the question: What is a monster? It is that which we cannot control. It is a sublime notion, and also somewhat archaically reliant upon a belief in fate. This was not evident in the first edition of her *Modern Prometheus*, which was written under Percy Shelleys's supervision and politics, but by 1831, Mary had become confident in her own individual vision: "Fate replaces individual choice in the 1831 edition, a revision which is heavily underscored by Mary's enrollment of nature as a giant force, as implacable as the monster. In the 1818 version, Victor saw the glacier at Chamonix only as a wonderful spectacle; in that of 1831, he is aware of 'the blind working of immutable laws'...."[xx]

It was these "immutable laws" that I sought. Raised, like most other readers, on the 1831 edition that was ultimately Mary's final revision of a Romantic manifesto, I could revel in the landscaped prose, but not really understand it from the sheltered quarters of my bedroom walls. But today, seeing the scenes for myself, I finally got it.

When Victor flees Belrive for Chamonix, he seeks the spiritualism unfounded within science: "The weight upon my spirit was sensibly lightened as I plunged...deeper in the ravine of Arve. The immense mountains and precipices that overhung me on every side, the sound of the river raging among the rocks, and the dashing of the waterfalls around spoke of a power mighty as Omnipotence—and I ceased to fear or to bend before any being less almighty than that which had created and ruled the elements."[xxi] Invigorated by the scenery, Victor feels himself part of this Omnipotence, since he has created life, but he is rudely awakened by the weather and by his creation.

I found the Alps moody. When it is sunny, the snow is glaring and luminescent, making the peaks underneath radiate with an omnipotent quintessence. When it rains, they become dark, stark, and veiled with misty and solemn judgment. The rain approaches slowly, misting over the aiguilles, the condensation gradually taking on the mountains' hues, until they blend together in sfumato ghostliness.

While I believe this a daily climate cycle, Victor reads this moodiness as a verdict on his actions, and finds nature—especially within the deified Mont Blanc—apathetic: "...All of soul inspiriting fled...dark melancholy clouded every thought. The rain was pouring in torrents, and thick mists hid the summits of the mountains, so that I even saw not the faces of those mighty friends."[xxii]

Chamonix was also an escape for Mary and her family. When Claire learned she was with Byron's child, the family retreated to the mountain village, where distance from Byron would allow them to plan around his growing disinterest. Traveling by foot and mule, it took the family three to four days to traverse the 82 kilometers between the Villa and the valley. This trek largely informed Mary's novel, including a night in Plainpalais, where the Creature's first murder occurs, and provided Victor's route.[xxiii]

There are many ways to follow Victor from Geneva to Chamonix, but perhaps the quickest and most efficient is with the Key Tours S.A. company,[xxiv] which offers routes comparable to that of Frankenstein's journey through the countryside. Via the bus' panoramic windows, what little is left of the Plainpalais forest can be glimpsed, including the Mont Salève cliffs the Creature traversed in twenty minutes, and L'Arvre's silty grey rapids rushing under roadways, railways, and bridges.

In the background, the Alps reign with rolling green hills that gradually fade into snow-dusted crags until the stark white of Mont Blanc bleaches the landscape of Chamonix, which Frankenstein describes as entering a different world: "The high and snowy mountains were its immediate boundaries, but I saw no more ruined castles and fertile fields. Immense glaciers approached the road; I heard the rumbling thunder of the falling avalanche and marked the smoke of its passage. Mont Blanc, the supreme and magnificent Mont Blanc, raised itself from the surrounding aiguilles, and its tremendous dome overlooked the valley."[xxv]

At 4,810 meters (15,781 feet above sea level),[xxvi] Mont Blanc is Western Europe's highest mountain, and its thick and endless sheets of snow and ice, punctuated by shadowy aiguilles, make it a living poem of beauty and terror. No wonder Shelley chose it as the subject of his existentialism, and Mary chose it as her novel's omnipotent patron saint.

Tourists can view Mont Blanc's summit by taking a lift to L'Aiguille du Midi's hiking station, then catching "The Rocket," a sonic elevator that shoots jam-packed tourists up and out on a viewing platform at the White Mountain's peak. From here, the view is sublime, and—despite being riddled with tourists taking pictures and ooo-ing and ah-ing—it is a lonely experience. Climbers scaling the mountain look like periods in an ever-winding ellipsis through time, part of which we all punctuate, including the tourists here in 20— and the Shelleys in 1816. It is in this eternal static that Victor finds comfort: "I had visited it frequently during my boyhood. [Now]...: *I* was a wreck, but naught had changed in those savage and enduring scenes."[xxvii] However, Victor's pilgrimage did not include a scaling of the mountain, but a descent to its moving glacier, Mer de Glace, where he is accosted with the horrible truth that *everything* has in fact changed, and *he* changed it.

The Shelleys and Frankenstein had to descend Montenvers to the Mer de Glace by mule, a trek so unsteady and precipitous that Shelley almost fell down the mountain. The glacier was well worth the peril, as he described in a letter: "On all sides precipitous mountains, the abodes of unrelenting frost, surround this vale: their sides are banked up with ice and snow, broken, heaped high, and exhibiting terrific chasms.... The waves are elevated about 12 or 15 feet from the surface of the mass, which is intersected by long gaps of unfathomable depth, the ice of whose sides is more beautifully azure than the sky.... One would think that Mont Blanc, like the god of the Stoics, was a vast animal, and that the frozen blood for ever circulated through his stony veins."[xxviii]

Fortunately, that path has been made easier for tourists. From Chamonix, a train takes visitors up 1,913 m (6,276 feet)[xxix] within a half-hour to the Montenvers train station, where a lift takes visitors down the vale to the moving glacier.

In the previous quote describing Victor's arrival to Chamonix, he mentions seeing the icy-sea from his lodgings, but it has not been visible from the village since 1820, and has shrunk about 2 km (1.24 miles) since the 1850s.[xxx] Even so, it is still massive enough, 200 meters (656 feet) thick on average, that a cave, known as the Ice Grotto, can be drilled out every summer to allow exploration of the ice's inner beauty, with the bonus of a visual reference to the steady but imperceptible flowing of the glacier, which moves about 70 meters (0.04 miles) every year.[xxxi]

The Grotto is dazzling despite being filled with tourist cheese like ice-sculpted furnishings among carved-out bedrooms and kitchens, and even an overpriced photo opportunity with a St. Bernard. But, kitsch aside, the main attraction is the preternatural coloring inside the glacier. Outside, the glacier appears filmy—a pale blue emanating from underneath snow, dirt, rocks, and gravel—but inside the ice is the crystalline mixture of a sapphire robustness with aquamarine clarity.

Victor, of course, never experienced the ice's interior, but rather relished its exterior isolation: "...My heart, which was before sorrowful, now swelled with something like joy; I exclaimed, 'Wandering Sprits, if indeed ye wander, and do not rest in your narrow beds, allow me this faint happiness, or take me, as your companion, away from the joys of life.'" As if in answer, Victor "...suddenly beheld the figure of a man, at some distance, advancing towards me with superhuman speed. He bounded over the crevices in the ice, among which I had walked with caution...."[xxxii]

Victor's reunion with his creature is one of *Frankenstein*'s more crucial scenes. Right before the confrontation, he describes the area as a temple, with Mont Blanc looming supreme over Frankenstein and the vast sea of ice: "From the side where I now stood Montenvers was exactly opposite, at the distance of a league; and above it rose Mont Blanc, in awful majesty.... The sea, or rather the vast river of ice, wound among its dependent mountains, whose aerial summits hung over its recess...." Although Victor retreats to Chamonix to clear his conscience, the mountain's mysticisms seem to apathetically reflect his attempts to thwart nature back into his face, and damn him by reuniting him with his Creature.

While I've written above about the Alps' moodiness, I didn't witness this atmospheric judgment (as Victor saw it) until returning back to Chamonix on the Montenvers train. As the scenery became obscured by pouring rain, I thought about the conflict that transpired under the King of the Mountain's court: the Creature confides his gained sensibility and intellectual experiences to his Father, and in true bad-dad fashion, Victor disavows him, declares him a disappointment, and declares him a monster. That declaration not only damned the Creature to further crimes and mayhem, but to a reputation of infamy and further misunderstanding in our popular culture. In the Universal films, you travel through the Creature's eyes, watch his development toward monstrosity but with no clue to his inner workings—he remains practically deaf and mute to the audience. He is forever embryonic. In Branagh's adaptation, you get a sense of the inner travel; however, people seem to prefer a dumb brute. Having seen Mary Shelley's face flash on a TV screen at the train platform, I queried my tour guide about his knowledge of the Creature and Mont Blanc, and he thought I was referring to the Villa Diodati.

"No," I said. "*Frankenstein* was also set here—." He cut me off with a scoff, "Oh, yes, yes, the monster scales Mont Salève in twenty minutes, or something ridiculous like that." He then mused for a moment while helping an old woman onto the bus. "You know, the Universal monster films had the right idea. The public do not want a philosophical monster; the studios were right to mute him."

Were they? Was it because in the book the Creature was a lateral man with a story most people, even those who made him thus, wanted to ignore because it was uncomfortable to believe? His world isn't big—his society is filled with a few people, none of whom gel with him, and therefore leads to an existence frustrated and exacerbated by misunderstanding and irresponsibility.

I chose to follow Victor rather than the Creature because the Creature's journey is not locked into sites like his creator, but has a geography of emotions—a child's map of his mental development that is very much Shelley's *conte philosophique* for Rousseau's thoughts on education, companionship, equality, and the noble savage. For a long time, he has no real sense of where he is and he is uninterested in the sublime. He is of nature, and he doesn't have to admire it or be against it, he is it.

But even so, there is the Black Forest between Ingolstadt and Geneva that shaped the Creature and made him the philosophical monster we all ignore. If I ever get to repeat this tour, it'll be the Creature's maps I draft and follow.

Oh, how late it is getting! How long this letter has grown, and how low the Bandol! I will close this with my wandering spirit sated and return to you soon.

Exhaustedly,

S—

ENDNOTES

[i] Already married, Percy could not legalize his relationship with Mary until his first wife committed suicide in December of 1816.

[ii] Mary Godwin was the daughter of Mary Wollstonecraft (the feminist authoress of *A Vindication of the Rights of Women* and of William Godwin, philosopher, anarchist, and author of the Gothic novel *William Godwin*. Both highly influential to Mary's generation.

[iii] Unfortunately, these establishments no longer stand.
Hay, Daisy. *Young Romantics: The Tangled Lives of English poetry's Greatest Generation*. New York: Farrar, Straus and Giroux. 2010. Amazon Kindle edition. Location 1628-36, Paragraph 2.

[iv] Shelley, Percy and Mary. *History of a Six Weeks Tour Through a Part of France, Switzerland, Germany, and Holland: With Letters Descriptive of a Sail Around the Lake of Geneva and of the Glaciers of Chamouni*. London: T. Hookham, Jun and C. and J. Olliver. 1817. Pp. 96-97.

[v] Ibid., Pp. 98-100.

[vi] Lord Byron's physician, Dr. John Polidori, was inspired by this bet to write *Le Vampyre*, which would go on to inspire other vampire works like Bram Stoker's *Dracula*.

[vii] From its publication in 1818, Frankenstein went through two more revised editions. The first was heavily edited by Percy Bysshe Shelley, who as a result was thought to be the book's anonymous author for several years. Mary Shelley's father, William Godwin revised it for re-publication in 1821, and finally, in 1831, Mary got the last word, revising the book to her mature beliefs and giving the book its final intellectual resonance, as well as perpetuating the romantic legend around the novel's birth: Seymour, Miranda. *Mary Shelley*. New York: Grove Press. 2000. Pp. 335;406-407.

viii Shelley, Mary. *Frankenstein. Frankenstein, Dracula, Dr. Jekyll and Mr. Hyde: With an Introduction by Stephen King.* New York: Signet Classic. 1978. Pp. ix-x.

ix Ibid. P. x.

x Ibid. P. xi.

xi This nice little moniker came courtesy of British poet Robert Southey, who saw the works of Lord Byron, Keats, and the Shelleys as highly rebellious and blasphemous, and termed them Satanic in his 1821 poem *A Vision of Judgement.* The term fit. "Satanic School." *Wikipedia, The Free Encyclopedia.* Wikimedia Foundation, Inc. 11 Dec 2011. Web. 8 Mar 2012. http://en.wikipedia.org/wiki/Satanic_School

xii Shelley, Mary. *Frankenstein. Frankenstein, Dracula, Dr. Jekyll and Mr. Hyde: With an Introduction by Stephen King.* New York: Signet Classic. 1978. P. 40.

xiii Habrich, Christa and Hofmann, Siegfried. Trans. Nicolas H. Llyod. *The German Museum of the History of Medicine in Ingolstadt.* Press Office of the City of Ingolstadt. 1991. Pp. 9-21.

xiv Shelley, Mary. Frankenstein. *Frankenstein, Dracula, Dr. Jekyll and Mr. Hyde: With an Introduction by Stephen King.* New York: Signet Classic. 1978. P. 53.

xv Ibid. P. 48.

xvi Habrich, Christa and Hofmann, Siegfried. Trans. Nicolas H. Llyod. *The German Museum of the History of Medicine in Ingolstadt.* Press Office of the City of Ingolstadt. 1991. P. 103.

[xvii] "Villa Diodati." *Wikipedia.* http://en.wikipedia.org/wiki/Villa_Diodati. Accessed August 15, 2010.

[xviii] The creature's murders happen mostly around Geneva's perimeter: Victor's baby brother William is murdered in the forests of Plainpalais, as is their servant Justine, (hung for the former crime, having been framed by the Creature). Victor's new bride, Elizabeth, is throttled the night of their honeymoon in Evian. Only one murder occurs abroad in Ireland, when the Creature kills Victor's companion, Henry Clerval.

[xix] "Mont Blanc: Lines Written in the Vale of Chamouni" was first published in the travelogue *A History of a Six Weeks Tour Through a Part of France, Switzerland, Germany, and Holland: With Letters Descriptive of a Sail Around the Lake of Geneva and of the Glaciers of Chamouni.* Published in 1817, it would be the only published collaboration of the couple, and collects letters and journals of their two Grand Tours together. Many of the descriptions and sentiments here would be repeated in *Frankenstein.*

[xx] Seymour, Miranda. *Mary Shelley.* New York: Grove Press. 2000. P. 407.

[xxi] Shelley, Mary. *Frankenstein. Frankenstein, Dracula, Dr. Jekyll and Mr. Hyde: With an Introduction by Stephen King.* New York: Signet Classic. 1978. Pp. 90.

[xxii] Ibid. P. 92.

[xxiii] Accounts of this trek are depicted in the letters of the Shelley's *History of a Six Weeks Tour Through a Part of France, Switzerland, Germany, and Holland: With Letters Descriptive of a Sail Around the Lake of Geneva and of the Glaciers of Chamouni.* London: T. Hookham, Jun and C. and J. Olliver. 1817.

[xxiv] The tour group also arranges for all your ticketing and transportation needs, as well as a nice, Swiss lunch so your time is utilized more sightseeing than standing in lines.

[xxv] Shelley, Mary. *Frankenstein. Frankenstein, Dracula, Dr. Jekyll and Mr. Hyde: With an Introduction by Stephen King*. New York: Signet Classic. 1978. P. 90.

[xxvi] Chamonix*net. "Mont Blanc Climb." Chamonix Networks. http://www.chamonix.net/english/mountaineering/mt_blanc_climb.htm. Accessed September 18, 2013.

[xxvii] Shelley, Mary. *Frankenstein. Frankenstein, Dracula, Dr. Jekyll and Mr. Hyde: With an Introduction by Stephen King*. New York: Signet Classic. 1978. P. 90.

[xxviii] Shelley, Percy and Mary. *History of a Six Weeks Tour Through a Part of France, Switzerland, Germany, and Holland: With Letters Descriptive of a Sail Around the Lake of Geneva and of the Glaciers of Chamonui*. London: T. Hookham, Jun and C. and J. Olliver. 1817, Pp. 166-167.

[xxix] "Chemin de fer du Montenvers [sic]." *Wikipedia*. http://en.wikipedia.org/wiki/Montenvers_Railway Accessed September 18, 2013.

[xxx] Nussbaumer, S. U., H. J. Zumbühl, and D. Steiner (2007): Fluctuations of the Mer de Glace (Mont Blanc area, France) AD 1500-2050. Part I: The history of the Mer de Glace AD 1570-2003 according to pictorial and written documents. *Zeitschrift für Gletscherkunde und Glazialgeologie*, 40(2005/2006), 5-140. http://www.geo.uzh.ch/~snus/publications/dipl_summary.pdf Accessed August 18, 2010.

xxxi Chamonix*net. "Mer de Glace." Chamonix Networks. http://www.chamonix.net/english/sightseeing/mer_de_glace.htm. Accessed September 18, 2013.

xxxii Shelley, Mary. *Frankenstein. Frankenstein, Dracula, Dr. Jekyll and Mr. Hyde: With an Introduction by Stephen King.* New York: Signet Classic. 1978. Pp. 94.

AFTERWORD

While these letters have already enjoyed previous publication, first online in three installments at Ann and Jeff Vandermeer's *Weird Fiction Review*, second as a complete piece in Zoetic Press' *Nonbinary Review: Issue #2 Frankenstein*, I have always wanted to see them as they were intended: delivered into the hands of Dear R— as a physical manifestation of ink and paper, and dispatched as such in time for the Bicentennial of that haunted summer in 1816 when Mary Shelley conceived *Frankenstein*. Because I know you can very well read these letters in these other avenues for free, I have decided to make this an artifact. This chapbook is only available as a limited edition of 200 copies, and will only be for sale from June 18, 2016 to February 18, 2017, to represent the nine months it took for Shelley to compose her first draft. Thanks to the designing help of Yves Tourigny, I have been able to offer up such a tribute, and to all my Dear R—'s who have purchased this chapbook, I thank you.

Even though "Wandering Spirits" is a relatively small piece, it was birthed with great pains and over a long duration. Fortunately, it has had many loving Godmothers and Godfathers who helped midwife it into the world. Cheryl Morgan, Adam Mills, Lise Quintana, and Allie Marini all helped it reach its full publication potential, while Stacy Froeschner, Lesli and Bill Green, Molly Tanzer, Jesse Bullington, Orrin Grey, J. T. Glover, Moco and Maize Steinman-Arendsee, and Jason Heller were all first readers and offered great encouragement for this piece to breathe and realize its own wail in the world.

After "Wandering Spirits" was published, I would have forgotten about it like I do everything I write, if it hadn't been for the constant championing and promotion of the work by Scott Nicolay. In fact, it is thanks to Scott that I met Yves Tourigny, and that my notion of a chapbook has come to pass.

Last, but never least, my gratitude and thanks go out to my husband Joshua Johnson, who obligingly allowed me to transform our honeymoon on the Côte d'Azur into a frenzied literary scavenger hunt among the Alps, and to my parents, Joseph Chambers and Dr.

Sonja Chambers, who never denied me a book and thus nurtured my vocation as we know it.

Obviously, the travels herein are incomplete. Between the Creature and Victor Frankenstein, they visited over 37 cities within 15 countries. Having only limited resources and time, I could only manage three cities within three countries. Even so, the rapidity with which Shelley and her Creation's sublimity was revealed to me has developed an obsessive curiosity to travel further within Mary Shelley's *Frankenstein*, that is if the Wandering Spirits will allow me.

ABOUT THE AUTHOR

Selena Chambers' fiction and non-fiction have appeared in a variety of venues including *MungBeing* magazine, *Clarkesworld*, *The Nonbinary Review*, *Tor.com*, *Bookslut*, *Cassilda's Song* (Chaosium, 2015), and *The Last Session* (Dunhams Manor Press, 2016). Her work has been nominated for a Pushcart, Best of the Net, and the Hugo and World Fantasy award. She is currently co-authoring with Arthur Morgan, a travel guide to *Steampunk Paris* (Pelekenisis), forthcoming soon.

You can find her online at her:

Website: www.selenachambers.com,
Facebook: https://www.facebook.com/Twiggsnet,
Twitter: @BasBleuZombie.

19790372R00032

Printed in Great Britain
by Amazon